WONDER
STARTERS

RICHARD BINNALL (handwritten)

Bees

Pictures by TANCY BARAN

Published by WONDER BOOKS
A Division of Grosset & Dunlap, Inc.
A NATIONAL GENERAL COMPANY
51 Madison Avenue   New York, N.Y. 10010

About Wonder Starters

Wonder Starters are vocabulary controlled information books for young children. More than ninety per cent of the words in the text will be in the reading vocabulary of the vast majority of young readers. Word and sentence length have also been carefully controlled.

Key new words associated with the topic of each book are repeated with picture explanations in the Starters dictionary at the end. The dictionary can also be used as an index for teaching children to look things up.

Teachers and experts have been consulted on the content and accuracy of the books.

Published in the United States by Wonder Books, a Division of Grosset & Dunlap, Inc., a National General Company.

ISBN: 0-448-09655-2 (Trade Edition)
ISBN: 0-448-06375-1 (Library Edition)

Printed and bound in the United States.

There goes a bee.
The bee is flying
to the flowers.

1

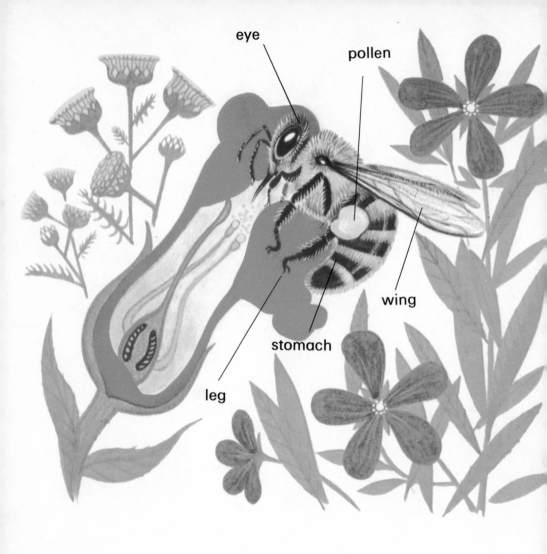

eye

pollen

wing

stomach

leg

The bee is taking food
from the flower.
It keeps pollen on its legs.
2

Now the bee is on another flower.
It gets nectar from the flower.
It puts nectar in its stomach.

3

The bee flies home.
Its home is a beehive
Lots of bees live in the hive.

4

The bee goes into the hive.
The hive is a big box.

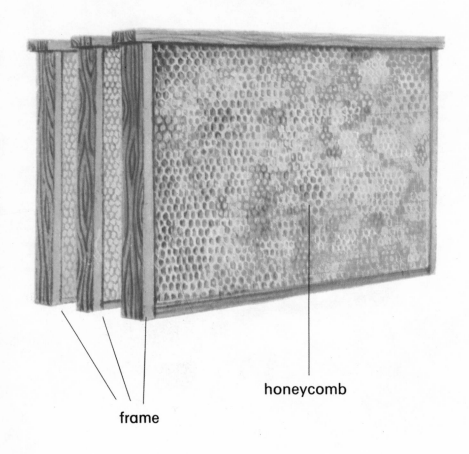

frame

honeycomb

There are honeycombs in the box.
A honeycomb has little cells.
6

Bees made the cells.
Some cells are for bees' eggs.
Some are for keeping food.

Most bees are worker bees.
They do all the work.
A few bees are called drones.
Drones are male bees.

8

This worker bee is making honey.
It makes honey from nectar.
Nectar comes from flowers.

9

Some bees put honey in cells.
Some bees make wax.
They put wax lids on the cells.

There are baby bees in some cells.
Worker bees feed the babies.
They give them honey.

11

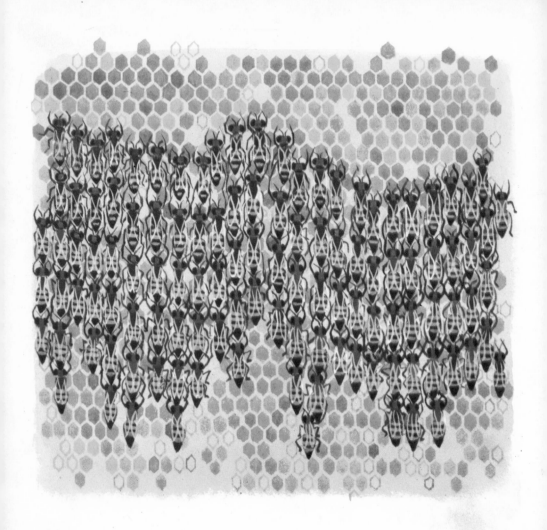

These bees are making new cells.
They make them with wax.
Each cell has six sides.

These bees have found food.
They do a kind of dance.
The dance tells the other bees
where the food is.

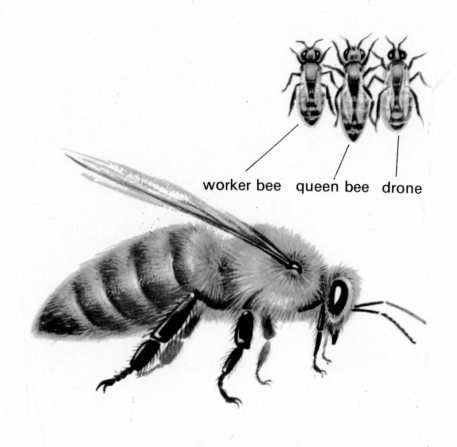

worker bee   queen bee   drone

This is the queen bee.
She is very big.
She does no work.

One day the queen flies out.
Drones chase her.
The fastest drone
becomes her mate.

Now the queen can lay eggs.
She lays one egg
in every empty cell.

16

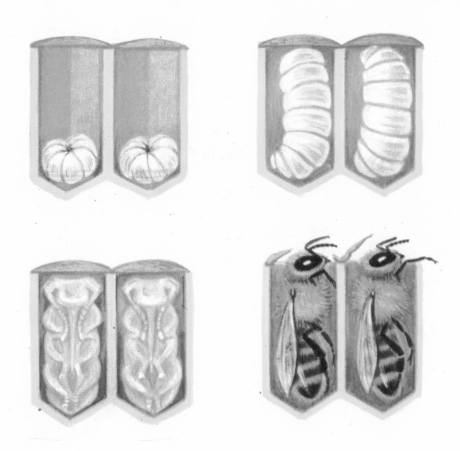

Each egg turns into
a larva.
Soon the larva turns into
a bee.

One larva turns into
a young queen bee.
Then the old queen flies away.
Many bees follow her.
18

Lots of bees are called a swarm.
The swarm finds a new hive.

19

The beekeeper
can take honeycombs out.
Smoke makes the bees sleepy.
They do not sting.

These bees do not live in hives.
They are wild bees.
They make honeycombs in trees.
They are found in India.

<u>See for yourself.</u>
Watch a bee on a flower.
Watch it take some pollen
from the flower.
22

Starter's **Bees** words

flower
(page 1)

stomach
(page 2)

pollen
(page 2)

nectar
(page 3)

eye
(page 2)

beehive
(page 4)

wing
(page 2)

honeycomb
(page 6)

23

cells
(page 6)

drone
(page 8)

frame
(page 6)

honey
(page 9)

egg
(page 7)

wax
(page 10)

worker bee
(page 8)

dance
(page 13)

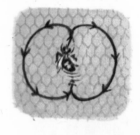

queen bee
(page 14)

beekeeper
(page 20)

larva
(page 17)

sting
(page 20)

swarm
(page 19)

wild bees
(page 21)